500 Dad Jokes

Funny, Clean, and Corny. The Best Dad Jokes to Tell Your Kids

Written by: Nina Riddle

Table of Contents

Dad Jokes 3

Knock Knock Dad Jokes 71

Dad Jokes

Why do most birds fly south for the winter? *They don't know how to drive.*

Why don't pandas get invited on canoe trips? *Instead of bringing paddles they bring pandamonium.*

What do you call a pony that sang for so long she lost her voice? *A little hoarse.*

What should a cowboy do if his ranch floods? *Start raising seahorses.*

Why didn't the ghost come to the dance? *Because he had no-body to go with him.*

What do you call a dry piece of cake? *A Sahara Dessert.*

Why don't thermometers go to college? *They've already got multiple degrees.*

What do wizards eat when they go to the beach? *Sandwitches.*

What species of fish always says her prayers before bed? *An angelfish.*

Why did the ferret get a job as a used car salesman? *He wanted to be a weasel.*

Why do football players like a lot of cereal for breakfast? *Because they get to eat it from a super bowl.*

What country makes the best winter jackets? *Chile.*

Which country do dogs avoid visiting because it's run by cats? *Fleegypt.*

What do frogs sit on at a restaurant? *Toad stools.*

Why aren't astronauts allowed to bring chewing gum into outer space? *NASA doesn't want them to get stuck up there.*▢

Why don't anchovies shake hands after they lose a game? *They're too salty.*

What did the almond farmer's wife say to her husband when he wouldn't stop humming? *"Cut it out, you're driving me nuts."*

Why do tall people make good astronomers? *They have high hopes.*

What did the bathroom say to the kitchen when the Titanic hit the iceberg? *"I had a sinking feeling that was going to happen."*

What do rhinos eat for breakfast? *Hornflakes.*

Where did the television go for Spring Break? *To a remote location.*

What did the lemon send back his fajitas? *The restaurant was out of sour cream.*

Why don't omelets go to college? *They can't pass their high school eggzams.*

What vegetable should you never give to people who have problems swallowing? *Artichoke.*

Why do chickens never drown? *They're eggcelent swimmers.*

Why did the nectarine do well in school? *His teachers all thought he was a real peach.*

Why do geologists love baseball? *It's played on a diamond.*

Where do hard drives hang their clothes? *In a storage closet.*

Why did Zelda bring a net and a jar to school? *She didn't want to lose the spelling bee.*

Why don't birds use computers? *They don't like windows.*

What should you do if you see an envelope on fire? *Stamp it out.*

What did the squid do when he felt sick? *He went to see the doctopus.*

Where do bulls and steers go on vacation? *Moscow.*

Why don't frogs tell jokes? *Because all they hear are crickets.*

Why did Aunt May divorce Uncle Ben? *She discovered he was an anteater.*

Which country has the most Grandmasters at Chess? *The Check Republic.*

What do gymnasts wear instead of makeup? *Flipstick.*

Which people make the best sprinters? *Russians.*

Why don't skunks make very good soldiers? *They're bad at taking odors.*

Which country always helps their friends when they move? *Packistan.*

What kind of snake do mechanics keep as a pet? *Windshield vipers.*

What did the suit salesman say to Albert Einstein after he tried on a tuxedo? *"You're looking smart."*

How do you put baby NASA scientist to sleep? *Sing her a song and rocket her back-and-forth.*

Why did the koala leave the zoo? *He couldn't bear it any longer.*

Why did was the beluga invited to the Royal Wedding? *He was the Prince of Whales.*

Why couldn't the fish log into his email? *He forgot his bassword.*

How did the astronaut lose his LEGOs? *They got sucked into a block hole.*

Why did the dog bite the doctor? *He didn't want a cat scan.*

Why did the puddle lose his job? *He was all dried up.*

Why didn't the saxophone get a part in the school play? *He blew his audition.*

What kind of bread do lemons eat? *Sourdough.*

What did the skunk want for his birthday? *A new smell phone.*

Why are farmers good at shooting billiards? *They're handy with a cue-cumber.*

How do you make Indian food run faster? *Hurry powder.*

What do you call a group of dads hunting for house flies using rolled-up newspapers. *A SWAT team.*

What do you call a big white bird with a yellow beak that isn't very good at catching fish? *A pelicant.*

Why are old computers bad at chess? *They don't have the memory for it.*

Why did the roast turkey say to the taxi driver? *"THANKSforGIVING me a lift."*

Why didn't the fog show up for work? *He was feeling under the weather.*

What did the hotdog tell the hamburger when he was getting too far ahead of her? *"Slow down and let me ketchup."*

What is a cat's favourite dessert? *Chocolate mouse.*

Why wasn't the polygon invited to the shape party? *He was a square.*

What do ghouls eat for Sunday dinner? *Ghost beef.*

Why was the bird angry with his barber? *He didn't want to be a bald eagle.*

Why were the grapes sent to bed early? *They were starting to wine.*

Why don't crabs use social media? *Because they're hermits.*

What do you get when you cross a lizard with formal Japanese robe? *A kimono dragon.*

What do rabbits eat on their birthday? *Carrot cake.*

Why did the clown quit his job at the circus? *He broke his funny bone.*

What do you call a dog with a metal detector? *A gold retriever.*

What kind of dog guards a vampire's castle? *A bloodhound.*

What genre of music do they listen to on the space station? *Rocket roll.*

Why are cows always staring up at the night sky? *They like to look at the moooooooooon.*

Why did the skeleton visit the doctor? *He couldn't stop coffin.*

What's the best type of letter to get on a hot summer's day? *Fan mail.*

Why don't young children make good tennis players? *They don't like squash.*

Why did the anteater's program crash? *It had too many bugs.*

What did the spice rack say to cupboard when a chipmunk ran through the kitchen? *"I don't have thyme for this."*

How did Donald Dock acquire all his wealth? *He made a killing in the stork market.*

What did the butter knife say to the steak knife? *You're looking sharp.*

Why don't plumbers like to fix bathtubs? *The work is very draining.*

Why did the brain surgeon get a part time job at the phone company? *He was a good operator.*

Why was the annoying tree cut down? *He was throwing too much shade.*

What do you call an annoying person related to you by marriage? *A bother-in-law.*

What do snowmen tell door-to-door salesmen when they don't want to buy anything? *"There's snowbody here, go away!"*

Why do painters make good gunslingers? *They're fast at drawing.*

What color did the dog paint his house? *Bark green.*

Why don't horses like spicy food? *It has too much of a kick.*

What is the only animal banned from all casinos in Africa? *The cheetah.*

What is dad's favorite snack? *Pop-corn.*

Where do fish sleep? *In tiny river beds.*

Why don't the wives of basketball players wear earrings? *They're tired of all the hoops.*▢

Why was the computer conference a failure? *The speakers weren't very good.*

Why was the hat so depressed? *He was in glove with a sock but she shooed him away.*

How do pirates fight underwater? *With a swordfish.*

Why aren't there any elves on Pluto? *It's a dwarf planet.*

Why do guinea pigs go on vacation? *Hamsterdam.*

Why don't mosquitos like baseball? *They feel uncomfortable when the players hit a fly ball.*

What do trains wear when they go jogging? *A tracksuit.*

What is the most expensive fish to stock your aquarium with? *Goldfish.*

What does the alarm clock do before he drinks his coffee? *He reads the snooze paper.*

Why did the octopus cancel his home phone? *He bought a shellfone.*

Why are cows good at killing vampires? *They've always got a steak handy.*

Which Sesame Street character spends all his time on the internet? *Cookie Monster.*

Why was the crab picked last for dodgeball? *He was a shrimp.*

Where do giant worms go on vacation? *The Big Apple.*

Why do lobsters make great judges? *They do well in claw school.*

Which species of bird makes the best carpenters? *Wood peckers.*

Why was the dog cut from the track and field team? *He was a bit husky.*

What was the dentist's favorite ride at the amusement park? *The molar coaster.*

What do wizards put on their pizza instead of basil? *Sage.*

What dog gets along the best with cows? *A bulldog.*

Did the grapes stop having children? *They got tired of raisin all those kids.*

Where does the world's deadliest assassin live? *The Blamazon Painforest.*

Why did the pig purchase so much land around the city? *He was a groundhog.*

What did mustard say when ketchup asked her out on a date? *"I relish the idea of spending time with a hot dog like you."*

What kind of tree do you never want to watch a sad movie with? *A weeping willow.*

What is the saddest spider? *The black widow.*

What do ogres eat for lunch? *Club sandwiches.*

Why did the spider sign up for high-speed internet? *She wanted to build a web page.*

What do you call the stinky nonluminous material that makes up 80% of the universe? *Fart matter.*

Why do pigs make good nurses? *They always know what oinkment to use.*

Why don't spoons like to go hiking? *They hate running into forks in the road.*

Why do villains make great novelists? *They're good at plotting.*

Why do stars like taking classes at college and university? *It makes them brighter.*

Why are minnows so intelligent? *They're always hanging out in a school of fish.*

Why aren't geese allowed on the same basketball team as turkeys? *Too many fowls.*

Why did the lantern fail his algebra test? *He was a bit dim.*

What do you call the cheaper version of a butterfly that looks the same but tastes a lot worse? *A margarinefly.*

What do skeletons order when they eat at a BBQ restaurant? *Spare ribs.*

What do fish listen to on the internet? *Codcasts.*

Why didn't the crab buy any Christmas presents for his friends? *He was shellfish.*

What's the secret to great airline food? *Just plane flour.*

What do astronauts read on the International Space Station? *Comet books.*

Why was the painting arrested for robbing the bank? *Because he was framed.*

Why did the brain surgeon ask his boss for a new computer? *It had a better operating system.*

What did the tomato say to the cucumber? *"Lettuce get out here before we end up in the chopper."*

What happens when two loaves of bread get married? *Someone gives a toast.*

How did the muskrat ask the beaver on a date? *"Do you want to gopher coffee?"*

What did the dentist say when the astronaut came in for a cleaning? *"You've got a great molar system."*

?

Why didn't the blanket go to jail? *He was found not quilty.*

Which British county manufactures the most doorbells? *The United Dingdom.*

What do you call a mountain that never explodes? *A volcanot.*

What do you call it when two cows are sitting in a squad car watching the farmer's house? *A steak out.*

Which movie won best picture at the 1973 fish Oscars? *The Codfather.*

Which insect always does well in school? *Spelling bees.*

How don't bakers use Microsoft Excel? *It doesn't have the breadsheet features they're looking for.*

Why does bread make you fat? *Because if you eat too much you'll loaf around all day.*

How did the ball of yarn get a job at the bank? *She pulled some strings.*

What do you call it when Dad takes off his socks and stinks up a hot room? *A feet wave.*⁇

How do broken electronics like their eggs? *Fried.*⁇

What do call a cloud that's out of breath? *Winded.*

What did the cob of corn ask Santa for? *World peas.*

What's a snake's favorite course in school? *Hissssstory.*

What is Jupiter's favorite board game? *Moonopoly.*

What's a duck's favorite snack? *Cheese and quackers.*

What do indecisive people use to protect themselves from the rain? *An ummmmmmmmmmmbrella.*

Why was father upset with mother? *She was being mum about where she wanted to go for dinner.*▢

What do dogs like Scottish music? *The love any song with wag pipes in it.*

What do deaf people drink on a hot day? *Hearingade.*

Why couldn't the computer get a job? *It was bad with applications.*

What color of fire truck did the zombie want for Christmas? *"Fright red."*

Why are kitchens good at math? *They have a lot of counters.*

What do you call someone who is obsessed with space? *An astronut.*

What do you call someone from Austria who takes care of sheep for a living? *A German shepherd.*

What ocean mammal weighs 3,000 pounds, leaves a slimy trail, and takes forever to get anywhere? *A beluga snail.*

Why can't shoes use computers? *They don't know how to boot them.*

What did the two gardeners serve for desert at their marriage reception? *A wedding rake.*

Why did Bruce Wayne quit his baseball team at age 7? *He was afraid of bats.*

What do karate fighters wear under their clothes? *Boxer shorts.*

What do you call a river that gets warmer until it tumbles off a cliff? *A hotterfall.*

How do planets clean themselves? *They take a meteor shower.*

Where do polar bears keep their money? *Snow banks.*

Why did the magnets get married after only one date? *They were attracted to each other.*

Why did the gorilla get detention? *He was monkeying around in class.*

What do you call a hamburger with two carrots sticking out of it? *Horned beef.*

How do hornets send letters to their grandparents? *Bee-mail.*

Why was the cockroach asked to leave the party early? *She was being a pest.*

Why didn't the teddy bear want any dessert? *He was stuffed.*

What did Mrs. Clause say when Santa asked her if she wanted to go for a walk? *"No thanks, it's raining deer."*

Where does a pig do his summer reading? *In the hammock.*

Why are ghosts not allowed into comedy clubs? *They always boo the comedians.*

Why are shoes so bad at public speaking? *They've got nothing to talk aboot.*

Why was the heron fired from his construction job? *The guy who hired him thought he was a crane.*

What do you call it when tropical trees start swaying in the wind? *The palm before the storm.*

Why did the flashlight fail her final exam? *She wasn't bright enough.*

What do you get when you cross an Roomba with a rhino? *A robotceros.*

Why do birds make great doctors? *They always know what tweetment to recommend.*

What do you call a seven-foot astronaut who farts in his space suit? *A gas giant.*

What did the French chef say to the duck? *"What's up, mon-goose?"*

What do mice say when they lose at checkers. *Rats!*

Where do Spanish people study astronomy? *At the lunaversity.*

What do you call a goofy wizard who spends a lot of time at the gym? *A Huffletuff.*

What is the karate kid's favorite drink? *Fruit punch.*

What is a tiger shark's favorite kind of sandwich? *Peanut butter and jellyfish.*

What do you call a flu that goes around in the first month of summer? *A junebug.*

Which country always makes a good deal in trade negotiations? *Fairaguay.*

What time in the morning does the bakery open? *Just after bunrise.*

What do cowboys eat for breakfast?
Western omelets.

Why don't cats make very good space aliens? *They don't like flying saucers.*

Why do banks on military bases have lots of security cameras? *They're afraid of tank robbers.*

What do horses put on their tuna sandwiches? *Hayonnaise.*

Why are clowns only funny in the winter? *Because during the summer their sense of humor is too dry.*

What did the pastry chef tell his apprentice when the cookies started to burn? *"Butter get on that."*

How do satellite repairmen like their eggs? *Scrambled.*

What did the jeans say to the t-shirt when their team was losing badly? *"We should give up, it's overalls."*

Why did the restaurant fire its website? *It wasn't a good server.*

Why don't fish and clams make good astronauts? *They don't like going into otter space.*

Why did the sled dog go on strike? *He was tired of being fed mush-rooms.*

Why don't email servers ever get hungry? *They eat a lot of spam.*

Why was the baseball player kicked off the team? *He went batty after losing the World Series.*

What do you call an elf that works at the library? *A bookshhhhhhh-elf.*

What did the police officer say to the snowman when he caught him robbing a bank? *"Freeze! I've got hairdryer and I'm not afraid to use it."*

What do you call a funnel cloud that quickly vanishes? *A boringnado.*

Why was the laundry sent down to the minor leagues? *He was all washed up.*

Why was the painting denied a bank loan? *It was overdrawn.*

Who is the cloud's favorite super hero? *The Flash of Lighting.*

Why did racecar driver put a big bet on himself to win the Indy 500? *He was carfident he would win.*

What's another name for flying fish? *Smallmouth Basshopper.*

What do you call a bug that likes to hide in shoes? *A sockroach.*

What sort of letters was the basketball player tired of getting? *Dunk mail.*

Why didn't the two town butchers get along very well? *There was a lot of beef between them.*

What do you call a depressed cruise liner? *A woe boat.*

Why did the candle quit his telemarketing job? *He was burned out.*

What happens to a salmon when it loses at a board game? *It turns into a jellyfish.*

Why did the cowboy have long hair? *Because he liked to tie it back in a ponytail.*

Why didn't the rat like working indoors? *He was a field mouse.*

What do you call alligator who works for the police department? *An investigator.*

Why is lettuce good at accounting? *It has real head for it.*

What species of bird make the best standup comedians? *Mocking birds.*

Why did the Russians send a dog into space? *Because they thought space travel was too ruff for humans.*

What did the Pharaoh say about his camel ride? *"It was a bit bumpy."*

What do you call a galaxy that's shaped like a horse? *The Milky Hay.*

How do people on vacation like their eggs? *Sunnyside up.*

Where country did the frog win a vacation to? *Flyland.*

What do you call a 40-year-old knight in shining armor? *Middle-aged.*

Where do fast people throw their garbage?
In the dash can.

How do you get a hamburger to admit to a crime? *You grill it until it confesses.*

What did the log cabin say after the tree told her she was beautiful? *"You're pretty wood-looking yourself."*

Why aren't oysters good at making friends? *When they meet new people their hands get clammy.*

Which sea creature makes the best tuba player? *The blow fish.*

What's the best species of snake to hire when you're building a house? *A boa constructor.*

What do you get when you cross a chicken with an elephant? *An animal that never forgets to look both ways before crossing the road.*

What do birds do when their IKEA furniture doesn't come with directions? *They wing it.*

What did the river say to the engineer? *"Wanna play some bridge?"*

What do rabbits use after they wash their head with shampoo? *Hare conditioner.*

Why was the palm tree sent to the Arkham asylum? *He was a real coconut.*

How does a gas giant keep its pants from falling down? *With an asteroid belt.*

What species of ants builds their homes inside a tree? *Carpenter ants.*

What is an astronaut's favourite snack? *A Mars bar.*

What is the gunslinger's favorite book? *Green Eggs and Blam.*

Why did nobody believe the tiger shark when he said his great-great-grandfather was Moby Dick? *It was a whale of a story.*

Why didn't the earthling show up to the party on Venus? *Bad atmosphere.*

What animal is banned from every restaurant? *The duck-bill platypus.*

Why did the broom get fired? *He was sweeping on the job.*

What do sports cars do on their day off? *Rewax in front of the TV.*

What do bullfrogs drink when they're trying to lose weight? *Diet Croak.*

Why are there always so many rabbits at a music award show? *They love hip-hop.*

Why don't baseball players ask for water when they go to a restaurant? *They've already got a pitcher.*

What do you call a goose that falls down a chimney? *A black swan.*

What do you buy a T-Rex for his birthday? *A lawn full of flamingos.*

What country is fun to visit because it can snow in the middle of summer? *The Weatherlands.*

Which country celebrates Halloween every month? *Booganda.*

What do computers do when they get a hole in their shoe? *Reboot it.*

What did the fog say to the grass? *"I mist you."*

What is black and white and swings from the trees with the greatest of ease? *A chimpanzebra.*

What do you call a squirrel with a bad attitude? *A chip-punk.*

Why are pirate-themed parties so dangerous? *Mom always goes overboard with the decorations.*

What did the apricot say to the prune? *"Want to go on a date?"*

When is the best time of day to eat candy? *Sour hour.*

Why did the sea urchin want to be an astronaut? *He always thought of himself as a starfish.*

What did the nightstand order when he went out for dinner? *Lamp chops.*

What sort of computers do babies use? *Naptops.*

Which country has the nicest dinnerware? *The United Plates of America.*

Why did the train love bubble gum? *Because it was a chew chew!*

What should you do if someone throws a bowling ball at your head? *Duck.*

What musical instruments do Labrador retrievers learn in school? *The trombone.*

What is a squirrel's least favorite type of nut? *A doughnut.*

Why didn't the zombie go to prom? *He didn't have a ghoulfriend.*

What did the skunk say when the porcupine hugged her? *Ow!*

Why do eggs make good fighter jet pilots? *They can scramble really fast.*

Why don't people with allergies go outside when there's a bad weather forecast? *It might start raining cats and dogs.*

Why was the banana rushed to the hospital? *He wasn't peeling well.*

What do volcanoes say on Valentine's Day? *I lava you very much.*

Why do bumblebees have such great hair? *They brush it every day with a honeycomb.*

What do scientists eat when their breath is stinky? *They eat an experimint.*

Why are cows afraid of trampolines? *They don't like milk shakes.*

Why do lobsters think fish are smart? *Because fish are always in a school.*

What's worse than finding a fly in your soup? *Finding half a worm when you bite into an apple!*

Why did the dill pickle need counseling and therapy? *It went through a jarring experience.*

How do honey bees get to school in the morning? *They take the school buzz.*

Why did the blue jays get married? *They were tweethearts.*

Why should you never throw bread and peanut butter into the street? *You might create a traffic jam.*

How do you make friends with a squirrel? *Just sit there acting like a nut.*

Why was the raspberry late for dinner? *He got stuck in a traffic jam.*

What is a hurricane's favorite board game? *Twister.*

What do strawberries say when they can't pay their bills on time? *Sure looks like were in a jam!*

What time is it if a hippopotamus sits on your car? *Time to get a new car.*

What is the most harmless type of lion? *A dandelion.*

Why was 0 jealous of 8? *She could afford a nice belt.*

What was the first thing the rabbits did after they got married? *They went on a bunnymoon.*▢

How did Emma know it was time to visit the dentist? *It was tooth hurty.*

What is a bat's favorite sport? *Baseball.*

What do vampires eat for breakfast? *Blood oranges.*

What was the pirate's favorite letter? *The letter arrrrrrrrrrrrrrr!*

How old do snowmen live? Until they *turn into water.*

What did the table say to the spoon?
Nothing. Tables can't talk, duhh!

What do you call a tiny tree? *A fit-in-your-palm tree.*

Why did the stegosaurus cross the road?
Because there weren't any chickens around to do it for him.

Why was the bowl of noodles arrested and accused of being a spy? *They thought he was an impasta.*

What is a circuit board's favorite snack food? *Computer chips.*

What do judges wear to weddings?
Lawsuits.

Why don't ponies ever sing the anthem at sporting events? *They're always a little hoarse.*

Why don't oranges run in marathons? *They always run out of juice.*

What did sandstone say to the quartz? *Stop taking me for granite!*

Why are so many ducks employed as police detectives? *They always find a way to quack the case.*

Why did the cooking student eat her homework? *It was a piece of cake.*

Why do you always see policemen at a baseball game? *In case someone tries to steal home.*

Why do Harvard professors always wear sunglasses when they teach? *Because their students are so bright!*

What did the pickle say to the cucumber when their child puked on the floor? *You dill with it.*

Why was the textbook sad and depressed? *Deep inside he had a lot of problems.*

What did the concessions stand worker say to the Hamburglar? *Hey, that's nacho cheese!*

What does Jupiter listen to on the car ride to work? *Neptunes.*

What did the street say to the room? *Let's grab lunch. I'll meet you at the corner.*

Why did the chicken walk across the waterpark? *To get to the other slide.*

What did the plant say when the oak tree got into an argument with the table? *Leaf me outta this.*

How do dairy cows get travel around the country? *In a mooving truck.*

Why did the monkey wear a rainbow suit? *So he could hide in the Crayon factory.*

Why was the drum skit so sleepy? *He was beat.*

What did the blanket say to the feet when got in trouble? *Don't worry, kid, I got you covered!*

Why did Bobby bring a ladder on the first day of classes? *His mom told him to make sure he was prepared for high school.*

What happens when you put dollar bills in the freezer? *You get cold hard cash.*

Why didn't cheddar invite Swiss cheese to go golfing? *He always gets a hole in one.*

What type of cookies do astronauts eat in space? *Chocolate rocket chip.*

How do you know when the Man on the Moon has eaten supper? *The moon will be full.*

Why are old people so wrinkly? *They don't like being ironed.*

Why do professional golfers always wear two shirts? *In case they get a hole in one.*

What is a pig's martial art? *Karate, because he learned how to do the pork chop!*

What do you call a cow that doesn't know how to fly? *Ground beef.*

What do oceans do when they run into their friends at the mall? *They wave.*

Why did the reindeer get kicked out of school? *He couldn't even say the elf-abet.*

What is a tree's favorite soda? *Root beer.*

Why do calculators make great employees? *You can always count on them to show up for work.*

What do crocodiles do when there's been a murder? *They call the investigator.*

Why aren't digital watches any good at sports? *They don't have hands.*

Why don't horses make very good ballroom dancers? *Their shoes are made of metal and they've got two left feet.*

What did the mountain say after the boulder told a funny joke? *Wow, that was hill-arious!*

Why are bored people always throwing clocks out the window? *They want to see time fly.*

What do you call a sleeping Tyrannosaurus?
A dinosnore.

How did the sink know the toilet was getting sick? *Her face was flushed.*

What did the dinner plate say to the duck? *Don't worry about the bill, the food is on me.*

Where did paper go on vacation? *Pencilvania.*

Why didn't the couch want any ice cream for dessert? *He was already stuffed.*

What kind of shoes does a ninja wear? *Sneakers.*

What type of cereal can't hold a job? *Cornflakes.*

What do you call a toothless bear? *A gummy bear.*

What has thousands of ears but can't hear anything? *A cornfield.*

How can you tell if there's a rhino under your bed? *You smacked your head against the ceiling.*

Why were the professor's eyes always crossed? *His pupils were out of control.*

What type of dinosaur makes a great English teacher? *A thesaurus.*

What musical instruments did the dentist play in the orchestra? *A tuba toothpaste.*

Why don't you ever see any vampires in winter? *They don't like getting frostbite.*

Why did the mayor burn down the town hall? *He wanted to win a no-bell prize.*

Why did 6 call the police? *Because 7 8 9.*

Why did the tablet PC go to the hospital? *It had a virus.*

Why was the doctor mad at the nurse? *She lost his patients.*

How can you tell there's been a parrot on your fridge? *Feathers in the milk.*

Why aren't poltergeists good at lying? *You can see right through them.*

Can a cricket jump higher than an elephant? *Yes, because elephants can't jump!*

Why didn't the maple tree want to visit the dentist? *She was afraid she needed a root canal.*

Knock Knock Dad Jokes

Knock, knock

Who's there?

Geese

Geese who?

Geese what time it is HONK HONK HONK!

Knock, knock

Who's there?

Lettuce

Lettuce who?

Open the door and lettuce find out together.

Knock, knock

Who's there?

Fun

Fun who?

Fun two three o'clock, four o'clock rock.

Knock, knock

Who's there?

Butter

Butter who?

Butter open the door before I huff and puff and blow your house down.

Knock, knock

Who's there?

Wannabuya

Wannabuya who?

No, I said wanna buy a *shoe?* I found one in the street.

Knock, knock

Who's there?

Heart

Heart who?

Heart to hear what you're saying. You'll have to speak louder.

Knock, knock

Who's there?

Al

Al who?

Illusions of grandeur, now lower your expectations and let me in!

Knock, knock

Who's there?

Ron

Ron who?

Ron, ron, ron as fast you can, you can't catch me I'm the gingerbread man!

Knock, knock

Who's there?

Bev

Bev who?

Beverages for sale, how many do you want?

Knock, knock

Who's there?

Nanna

Nanna who?

None of your business. This is my house.
You tell me who YOU are.

Knock, knock

Who's there?

Mikey

Mikey who?

My key fell down the sewer, so can you open the door before I freeze to death?

Knock, knock

Who's there?

Olive

Olive who?

I don't know, probably that girl you keep making faces at.

Knock, knock

Who's there?

Doctor

Doctor who?

Sure I've got time for a couple episodes.
Load it up.

Knock, knock

Who's there?

Czech

Czech who?

Czech yourself before you wreck yourself.

Knock, knock

Who's there?

Boo

Boo who?

Are you crying? There's no crying in baseball!

Knock, knock

Who's there?

Nebraska

Nebraska who?

Nebraska ask a magician how he performs his tricks.

Knock, knock

Who's there?

Abby

Abby who?

A bee stung me and now my face is swollen.
Can I have some Benadryl?

Knock, knock

Who's there?

Robin

Robin who?

Robin the bank around the corner and I
forgot my getaway car, can I hide here for a
while?

Knock, knock

Who's there?

Adjust

Adjust who?

Adjust saw a UFO crash in your backyard.
Do you have a minute to talk about aliens?

Knock, knock

Who's there?

Ireland

Ireland who?

Ireland you money if you agree to a 7%
interest rate.

Knock, knock

Who's there?

Dishes

Dishes who?

Dishes the police. We have a warrant to search the property for extraterrestrials.

Knock, knock

Who's there?

Halibut

Halibut who?

Halibut you and me sign up for soccer this year?

Knock, knock

Who's there?

Moneys

Moneys who?

Moneys are sore because I went hiking yesterday and almost fell into a volcano.

Knock, knock

Who's there?

Kenya

Kenya who?

Kenya open the door, lass? Thar be a whole lot o' pirates out here, yarr.

Knock, knock

Who's there?

Alex

Alex who?

Alextricity ZAP ZAP ZAP!

Knock, knock

Who's there?

Ya

Ya who?

Nobody uses that anymore. Everyone's using Google now. Get with the program!

Knock, knock

Who's there?

Phillip

Phillip who?

Phillip with premium gas, please. The cheap stuff might ruin the engine.

Knock, knock

Who's there?

Atch

Atch who?

Oh I'm sorry, do you have a cold? I'll come back later.

Knock, knock

Who's there?

Wire

Wire who?

Wire you not opening the door? I gave you the password and everything. Did they change it? Is it not *smelly unicorn* anymore?

Knock, knock

Who's there?

Bat

Bat who?

Bat you'll never guess my secret identity.

Knock, knock

Who's there?

Needle

Needle who?

Needle little help carrying a mattress up the stairs. How about you lend me a hand and I forget that 10 bucks you owe me?

Knock, knock

Who's there?

Iran

Iran who?

Iran home from school because it's good exercise and coach said if I don't practice more I'll never make the soccer team.

Knock, knock

Who's there?

Ooze

Ooze who?

Ooze that funny looking woman sleeping on the couch? She's not related to you is he?

Knock, knock

Who's there?

Waiter

Waiter who?

Waiter I get my hands on some good material, then we'll who's the comedian around here!

Knock, knock

Who's there?

Math

Math who?

Math potatoes and gravy delivery. Sign here or forfeit your chicken.

Knock, knock

Who's there?

Pie

Pie who?

Pie was thinking about getting an iguana as a pet. What do you think?

Knock, knock

Who's there?

Irish

Irish who?

Irish you a happy birthday and many more to come. Now where's the cake?

Knock, knock

Who's there?

Dozen

Dozen who?

Dozen anybody hear me knocking? I'm gonna die of exposure out here.

Knock, knock

Who's there?

Russian

Russian who?

Russian around out here and I crashed my car into a giant boulder. Can you call me a tow truck?

Knock, knock

Who's there?

Barbie

Barbie who?

Barbie Q repair man. I heard you have a problem with you propane and propane accessories.

Knock, knock

Who's there?

Amal

Amal who?

Amal in the west end is offering free shoes with the purchase of a bowling ball. Let's go check it out.

Knock, knock

Who's there?

Heaven

Heaven who?

Heaven seen that movie in forever. Let's make popcorn and watch it with the volume turned up really loud.

Knock, knock

Who's there?

Cargo

Cargo who?

No, cargo HONK HONK HONK, get outta my lane!

Knock, knock

Who's there?

Venice

Venice who?

Venice the best time to stop by and pick up that power drill I loaned you?

Knock, knock

Who's there?

Egg

Egg who?

Eggstremely annoyed you aren't opening the door. What am I, chopped liver?

Knock, knock

Who's there?

Candy

Candy who?

Candy the dog come outside to play? I brought my rabbit and put him on a cute little leash.

Knock, knock

Who's there?

Woo

Woo who?

Wow I haven't heard that song in forever.

Knock, knock

Who's there?

Guinea

Guinea who?

Guinea a break, man, it's my first day on the job.

Knock, knock

Who's there?

Spain

Spain who?

Spain to me why I shouldn't use my bulldozer to knock this door down.

Knock, knock

Who's there?

Odor

Odor who?

Odor from the boss, report to work at 7AM or find yourself a new job.

Knock, knock

Who's there?

Minneapolis

Minneapolis who?

Minneapolis will fall if you smack the fruit tree with a sledge hammer.

Knock, knock

Who's there?

Cod

Cod who?

Cod in a bad snowstorm and I was wondering if I could use your phone.

Knock, knock

Who's there?

Aries

Aries who?

Aries a reason why your house is so ugly?

Knock, knock

Who's there?

Armenia

Armenia who?

Armenia everything I said last night about your new wardrobe and I don't think those colors make you look like a clown. Unless that's what you were going for. In that case you nailed it.

Knock, knock

Who's there?

Utica

Utica who?

Utica the kids to school and I'll pick them up.

Knock, knock

Who's there?

Celery

Celery who?

Celery isn't high enough. So if I don't get a raise I gonna quit.

Knock, knock

Who's there?

Honey comb

Honey comb who?

Honey comb your hair. You look like a homeless buffalo.

Knock, knock

Who's there?

Taipei

Taipei who?

Taipei 200 words-a-minute and you get can a job as a court reporter.

Knock, knock

Who's there?

Howie

Howie who?

H-*owie* I stubbed my toe on the door because you didn't open it fast enough.

Knock, knock

Who's there?

Noah

Noah who?

Noah any good mechanic to get my car fixed? It won't start and my tires are missing.

Knock, knock

Who's there?

Bud

Bud who?

Bud is running out of my nose do you have any Kleenex?

Knock, knock

Who's there?

Claire

Claire who?

Claire the front hall. We got a fridge and a dining room table coming through here in about five minutes.

Knock, knock

Who's there?

Alaska

Alaska who?

Alaska the questions here, pal, you're in enough trouble as it is.

Knock, knock

Who's there?

Sherlock

Sherlock who?

Sherlock your door at night, you never know what's creeping about out there.

Knock, knock

Who's there?

Ho ho.

Ho ho who?

You need to work on your impressions if you're ever gonna make it as a mall Santa.

Knock, knock

Who's there?

Tennessee

Tennessee who?

Tennessee is a hard game. You need to be in great shape if you want to win a tournament. So you're in trouble, dad.

Knock, knock

Who's there?

Teddy

Teddy who?

Teddy is a great day for playing basketball. Let's make teams and reserve a court.

Knock, knock

Who's there?

Police

Police who?

Police open the door. It's raining and I forgot my umbrella.

Knock, knock

Who's there?

Hairy

Hairy who?

Hairy up and get ready, the movie starts in less than 30 minutes.

Knock, knock

Who's there?

Norway

Norway who?

Norway you're going to the mall dressed like that, mister.

Knock, knock

Who's there?

Luke

Luke who?

Luke through a telescope at night and you can see Saturn. It's the prettiest planet in the entire sky.

Knock, knock

Who's there?

Snow

Snow who?

Snow use, I forgot the password. You'll just have to trust me and unlock the door.

Knock, knock

Who's there?

Ben

Ben who?

Ben standing out here for thirty minutes waiting. What were you doing, dry cleaning a sofa?

Knock, knock

Who's there?

Arizona

Arizona who?

Arizona room in this kitchen for two dwarves and a frying pan. Call the real estate agent and tell her to look for a bigger house.

Knock, knock

Who's there?

Debbie

Debbie who?

Debbie a young man again would be nice, but old age has its advantages.

Knock, knock

Who's there?

Ya

Ya who?

No need to get excited, it's just me, Bob the mailman, and all I've got for you is flyers.

Knock, knock

Who's there?

Howl

Howl who?

Howl you know what I'm selling unless you answer the door?

Knock, knock

Who's there?

Justin

Justin who?

Justin the neighborhood smelling all the flowers and walking on your lawn. What are you up to?

Knock, knock

Who's there?

Texas

Texas who?

Texas and rent and too darn high!

Knock, knock

Who's there?

Theresa

Theresa who?

Theresa bald eagle sitting in my tree, want to see it?

Knock, knock

Who's there?

Goat

Goat who?

Goat see what all that ruckus is out back. It sounds like someone is juggling cats.

Knock, knock

Who's there?

Chile

Chile

Chile? It's colder than space out here. Now open up!

Knock, knock

Who's there?

Omar

Omar who?

Omar god, Becky, look at these shoes!

Knock, knock

Who's there?

Alpaca

Alpaca who?

Alpaca the food and you packa the clothes. We've got less than two hours before the hurricane get here.

Knock, knock

Who's there?

Madam

Madam who?

Madam broke and now the yard is flooding.
Can I borrow your vacuum cleaner?

Knock, knock

Who's there?

Scold

Scold who?

Scold outside, so you better let me in
before my fingers fall off.

Knock, knock

Who's there?

Thermos

Thermos who?

Thermos be some kind of way out of here, said the joker to the thief.

Knock, knock

Who's there?

Witches

Witches who?

Witches the best way to get to the park?
The bike path or through the garden?

Knock, knock

Who's there?

Radio

Radio who?

Radio or not it's time to go to school so grab your backpack and lunch bag.

Knock, knock

Who's there?

March

March who?

Martians are invading so you better let me and we'll make smores and watch the invasion on TV.

Knock, knock

Who's there?

Italy

Italy who?

Italy be all over for the roses if you don't open this door.

Knock, knock

Who's there?

Tank

Tank who?

You're welcome. This is a hard job and nobody appreciates me.

Knock, knock

Who's there?

Barry

Barry who?

Barry your treasure on a desert island if you want to hide it from the navy.

Knock, knock

Who's there?

Annie

Annie who?

Annie body home in there? I've got a barrel of monkeys and keg of orange juice.

Knock, knock

Who's there?

Figs

Figs who?

Figs your fence before it falls onto my property and crushes my daffodils.

Knock, knock

Who's there?

Aldo

Aldo who?

Aldo anywhere you want on vacation, except Cuba.

Knock, knock

Who's there?

Will

Will who?

Will you be my valentine?

Knock, knock

Who's there?

Jamaican

Jamaican who?

Jamaican me wanna buy some jerk chicken and some of those funny looking bananas.

Knock, knock

Who's there?

Roach

Roach who?

Roach you a nice birthday message on Facebook but I decided to deliver it in person. I know it's 6AM but *the early gecko gets the roach*. And cheap car insurance. So there. Happy birthday. How about some breakfast?

Knock, knock

Who's there?

Ken

Ken who?

Ken you turn down your music? My grandmother is super old and is trying to sleep.

Knock, knock

Who's there?

Wooden shoe

Wooden shoe who?

Wooden shoe like to buy some Girl Guide cookies? Only five dollars a box.

Knock, knock

Who's there?

Kansas

Kansas who?

How long Kansas go on? How long Kansas go on? How long Kansas go on? How long Kansas go on?

Knock, knock

Who's there?

Denial

Denial who?

Denial is a river in Egypt, silly, how could it be knocking on your door?

Knock, knock

Who's there?

Wendy

Wendy who?

Wendy saints go marching innnnnn!

Knock, knock

Who's there?

Stopwatch

Stopwatch who?

Stopwatch-a doing and open the door. I've got important news regarding your application to Hogwarts.

Knock, knock

Who's there?

Annie

Annie who?

Annie you want me to be. I'm a shapeshifter.

Knock, knock

Who's there?

Dwayne

Dwayne who?

Dwayne the pool before it gets too cold or it'll turn into a skating rink.

Knock, knock

Who's there?

Sasquatch

Sasquatch who?

Huh? How many sasquatches do you know?

Knock, knock

Who's there?

Vampire

Vampire who?

Vampire Strikes Back! (*Try and bite them*)

Knock, knock

Who's there?

Adore

Adore who?

Adore is the only thing keeping us apart. Let's knock it down!

Made in the USA
Columbia, SC
16 December 2018